child in the wings

Also by Nicola Bowery

Bloodwood (Bunda Press, 1996)
Goatfish (Bunda Press, 2007)
married to this ground (Walleah Press, 2014)

Walleah Press
PO Box 368
North Hobart
Tasmania 7002 Australia
ralph.wessman@walleahpress.com.au

Cover by Askepott Design
Cover photo by Nicola Bowery (Point Leo rock pools)
Set in Perpetua 12.5/15 by Ralph Wessman
Printed by Lightning Source, Melbourne

ISBN: 978-1-877010-12-5

child
in
the
wings

nicola bowery

Constituent
memories of a large memory.
Points of clarity in a mist, intermittently visible,
like a lighthouse whose one task
is to emit a signal.

Louise Glück
Faithful and Virtuous Night

this morning a blue balloon on the dam's edge

    is this the day childhood beckons?

once in a blue moon a blue moon lands
preens itself in the water
two blue moons on the dam's edge

    come back   come back

whose party is it?
how far has it flown this blue balloon
across forest wilderness, ploughed ground?

    remember ten years old the birthday party
    that wasn't
    the friendless girl with a stamp of polio
    no one came

once in a blue moon a blue moon lands
preens itself in the water

    and childhood beckons
    come back   come back

memory
        how it punches through
        part of a body neatly boxed away
        stored under earth

then suddenly a fist breaks out of its coffin
pierces the long-mouldering compost
pear tree leaves once orange and yellow

or the days it is softer
a seepage from a waterfall
long stilled and dried
with water traces only

seams in the rock the old fissures
from which memory now seeps
        through the skin

no wonder the Greeks called them rivers

    remembering and *forgetting*

called them

    Mnemosyne, Lethe

and the instruction was

    bathe in each of their waters
    drink from them both

the ancient tutelage

    drink from them both

and before remembering
there's the ur-trace of a body of water

they said
they said there was an interlude on an ocean liner

before childhood began to leave a scent

      there's an ocean that a baby is rocking on
      her baby eyes seeing waves perhaps

      three months old
      held tight on the deck by her mother's helper

      and is her tiny body soothed by the rocking in her blood

      the music of water?

like a beagle I go sniffing after the original scent
        like a beagle   I keep being side-tracked
the perfumes are complex
other creatures have overlaid them
and I keep sniffing for the original traces
        the map that I must myself have walked on
        in shoes of various sizes
my childish feet clothed in leather always leather
exuding the aromas of childhood
not the smell of the cow the shoe was cut from
        so   beagle   keep your nose
        pinned to the ground

and where's childhood?

here

here now

fresh-faced and quivering

what aches?

        remembering how she looked
        the girl with her polio-buckled leg
        and her stiff plain cheek
        her asking for a party
        and the party's gaping holes
        the balloons uninflated uncoloured airless

what aches?

        that the girl asked
        and I was the only one who answered
        perhaps the only one asked
        and the hole gaped wide
        no candle no cake no wishes no smile

        but the secret cemented and I lied
        inflated balloons and colours and dresses and giggles
        pass-the-parcel and pull the crackers
        party-time party-time

the ache of the lie

memory's flurries

     Mnemosyne's river
        frothing, glinting

     Lethe slurring
        Lethe's slurry

and the child that pops out
        now and then

            from under the blanket

Seaford
the gateway with PAX
carved on each stone pillar
        five years old you can read the words

cross the road
and first the ti-tree clumps
thick and shadowed
and sometimes a figure in the bushes
        and you hurry

then the brightness
sand and sea and sky
        wide and wide

and today the water's green and choppy
there'll be shells and seaweed skirts
        a chance of jellyfish bits

see that child there on the beach
three years old golden curls little round face
her swimming togs with the bobbly bits
dripping down her front almost to her
            chubby knees

and nothing else exists but the stocking net
she's staring into and its pearly catch
the four jelly blobs squidging there
all wet and glistening in the sun
            see her shining rapture

then the farm without a name
so it borrows the name of its place
Langwarrin
and it comes with 26 acres
a huge patch of thistles
a huge patch of potatoes
paddocks and bracken
a draught horse *Popeye*
a black pony *Tommy*
an unnamed dog
a house like a shack
candles and kero lanterns
a boiler for washing, a wringer
an outdoor loo with spiders
a front orchard
back orchard
and a thousand chickens

how and why did it land just here
this house beached like a boat

no waves beyond the undulations of grass
smallish trees, scrub across the road

the sea a long way off and the boat looking
out to it, looking out to sea

but not mournful, not like a beached whale
and the house not really boat-like

except all who sail in her
the Captain's cabin wedged in the middle

and it's here the sea abandons us
except it's winking from the horizon
a comfort but also desolate
a reminder of its distance
how it made hardly a splash
saying goodbye
but can't you still hear
the ripping sound in my heart?

and it's here we become a landlocked unit
anchored in nettles, spuds, chickens
the placid bay no longer at our toe-tips
our bodies no longer in that simple line
on the sand facing seawards
or curled in separate raptures with jellyfish
shark's purse, castle, bucket
the waves swallowing our voices
the sea reminding us
    you are minuscule

and now facing each other each of us is larger
inflated, facing inwards, landwards
becoming a land-locked unit
a family puzzled by its own significance

far cry
from the trim of a wave
on the bay's beach
the trace of her tiny foot
disappearing
as the tide rolls in

far cry
to the draught horse hoof
and its print on the dirt
in the potato patch
and who fell down?

memory
		like an invisible layer of clothing
		the extra membrane wrapped around the outer skin

like an aura you can enter from the inside only
		and only you can enter

a whiff of grieving
because our mother our father
had left their home countries

       a whiff of grieving
       because this is not England not Europe
       because the mountains are not mountains
       because the light is too brazen
       because the wattle is not a primrose
       because the gum trees are not oaks
       because green is grey and mustard yellow
       because the birds are too raucous

       a whiff of grieving
       because this is not their home country

the four of us girls 1 to 4
and often she jumbles our names
our mother
running down the scale
who can blame her
but of course I do
number 4
at the end of the run
blame her for muddling us
a child is such a bossy thing
and then there's the one too long after
to be on the scale
boy
and he blames no one

how the few stubborn images hold sway

      call them planets unblinking planets
      those pivotal beacons of memory

the few stubborn images

      unblinking planets
      staring out the lesser stars

but we were children then
        we all had childish minds
it seems we don't forgive ourselves for that

when my own star popped out later in the sky
        I watched the others carefully
they'd been blinking longer they must know something

still it feels treacherous speaking of how we were
        how we were in our childish constellations

someone says

> a memory is like a phantom limb
> part of your body once
> that can ache

and sometimes it burns with a strange heat

but still belongs

morning's rush for the train one of us always needs shouting at and I'm squashed middle back seat and it's three miles of gravel turning right into the last mile with the train line parallel on our left the race is on heart's clutch seeing the engine-smoke just in front or just behind and how badly I want to be on board on the rails and not jammed in this metal bubble our father whooping up the chase the slew and weave and scatter of stones but we're gaining on the puffing train as we always do and swing onto the tiny dirt platform how lonely it looks pinched out of the scrub and sometimes time enough to wave the red flag that's curled in a tin sleeve on the shed wall and practise Morse code even though the driver knows of course day after day and there's George the guard in his navy cap bending down from his steep iron step his hand stretched out to pull me up the smallest and his eye so kind and his grin I can't believe it and I keep looking at his eye and don't watch the gap so his hand is extra strong gripping pulling then he jumps out waves the green flag that has its own sleeve and George has warmed the metal sleeper things ready for our feet and I'm in the magic zone of the carriage with its spell of going somewhere so I can forget all the others to their windows I'm all alone with my nose on the glass and straight away I'm on the pony I want so much when I see those sandy tracks winding off into the bush and they always disappear round a corner when my pony's cantering nicely and who knows where I'll get to

horsehair
what no one in this family has a clue about
our mother surely once as a girl with ponies
but no one else hunts it out
that sweetness of horsehair scent
when you lift the mane and nuzzle there
where the hair springs out of the neck
      no one here has a longing for that
        what do they long for?

silly girls concussed blaming each other
the boom of the ground as they land
the draught horse hoof is all they see
at hoof level, its great thatch of hair
and I'm not there when they fall
but I know Popeye that placid giant
I know he'd hold his hooves still
while they're scooped out howling
and not his fault he's banished
his hoof prints lasting longer in the soil

I've never liked pink eyes piggish on a horse
see that one there see her mean streak
how she flares the pink of her nostrils
and flicks her rump   *watch out*
the horse is too close to my chest
too loved and feared
how do I take *horse* off my chest
and let you in
how do I let all of us breathe
so the horse can have his mouth to himself
smell the stirrups that flap of saddle
blow out pony I love your stubborn belly
horse you know me too well   all my trembles
be kind
a horse's eye   I love its liquid message

it's always someone else's
horse that is
this one unnerves me with his knowing
I'm weightless as a jockey   well I wish
how the horse hates the March fly
I dream and dream the perfect horse
and find him   once   and how I love and love
for a day   then his owner reclaims him
you can tell *she* was born in the saddle
and now I'm on a twitchy sour-faced mare
I wobble   my mother never thought
I needed lessons
I wear my biggest rictus grin and they say
how brave and daring
and race me down the gullies
pony don't roll me in the dam I know you want to
don't step on me kick me buck me trample me
don't scrape me off under that branch
I haven't reached the age of sweating
I ride on fear and it quickens from trot
to canter to gallop
I ride on that sweet sweet scent
of a sweating horse at a canter

Smokey with the iron mouth
the grey that runs away with me
free as a scudding cloud of smoke
we pelt up roads and pound round bends
me on his neck like a dizzy fly
and when he cuts the corners
I swivel on his wither
and he bolts through his home gate
and I'm swinging like a hammock under his neck
bumping against his steaming chest
subside on the dirt like a drop of his sweat
stunned to be still

see how memory scatters its debris
like on that beach the other day
flood-littered with trunks branches
foliage from the she-oaks way up river

their limbs sodden and dark-salted
a savage graffiti on the pale
blank page of the beach

that's what memory can do
even without storm weather
it can flood without warning
flooded by memories

can litter its wreckage
bruising what seemed innocent
innocent as sand

chewing

eschewing

chewing *es*

es

the unchewed

cud of childhood

there's the long table
which pulls us into our places
like a magnet
there's our father at the head
our mother facing him the other end
he talks the most
sister number 1 the next
both with loud voices
the rest of us sputter half
a sentence but the words wander
there's the food of course and it's good
our father makes a *Deutsche Witze*
and I laugh too hard to make sure
he knows I'm laughing
but the ham rind I'm chewing on
almost has me choking
and I punch it down quick
there's one of us holding her fork up
with nothing on it
like a dare
and there's a shadow round it
and I try not to see her flap her hankie
over her plate and how her sleeve-band bulges
so now there are the small weighing scales
they bring in to weigh the portions
and there's more silence
somehow the table keeps standing
with all its secrets
and we slip away

The kindness of the light streaming through the French windows.
At the dining room table my back's always to the windows wishing
it wasn't because I can't see the sea blinking on the horizon so I
face the long wall that's painted blue then charcoal then rusty red
and there's a picture of a violin and vase that fades, then the living
room wall gets knocked down so the room's made longer. A sea-
blue carpet says this part is living room and that dining, the wide
fireplace also rusty red and above it a large picture that goes very
brown from the smoke. Five brown figures men or women you
can't tell which dancing half-draped in long flowing things you
wouldn't say were dresses and their dance frightens me, their linked
arms and their half-nakedness. Creepy. Rude. Embarrasses me with
visitors. Like the faulty latch on the bathroom door and the soap
in a nest of grime on the sink's left upturned palm. The soapy glug
too round the plughole that I scrape out when my friend stays. The
kitchen is long and thin, has louvre windows, small bright red roses
outside pushing against the flywire. At one end what's called the
dinette with red lino on the tabletop same as the floor, breakfast the
only time except for the car we're all squeezed in. Piles of washing-
up by the sink. Baking bowls. Licked. From the living room a short
narrow hall like a dark tunnel to the rest of the house. Grope past
the two bedroom doors to the end the clunky door handle that
never gets fixed then thankfully light again and where I sleep a
closed-in verandah, more French windows, four of us then later
two sharing with the ping-pong table and the older ragged orchard
beyond. That's it.

over the road   over the road
head-high bracken and grey sand under

don't go there don't go

howls of spaniels up the hill in their bunker
the house all empty   emptied of dogs

don't go there don't go

watsonia white and pink pushing at the door
now closed

don't go there don't go

that woman whose hair flares red as flame
comes once a week with her bag of bones

don't go there don't go

and there's a hush in the wailing
where has she gone?

Frenchie they call her and the house the land
Frenchie's

don't go there don't go

and where to go?

up the pine tree and straddle the saddle
of a favourite branch, pine needles sticky on my
fingers, and the voices way below
lose their meaning on the travelled air

and where to go?
paint the Spanish beauty in her mantilla
mantilla, it sounds like music
an instrument she plays a long way off
but I draw her close up, her black lace

and where to go?
hide in the bracken at the paddock's end
hide under the green and lacy mantilla of bracken
its coolness, watch the ants in their tracings

and where to go?
go where no one else would think of going
under the pony's belly when there's rain and
thunder and the pony knows she has to offer shelter

memory
        hops and flits
        like a plump bossy bird

landing here and there squawking
        that time   that place

see the poop-spatters on that rock
        look at the swollen belly

how does it lift off into flight again
        with that gutful of stories

or is it a flightless bird
        grounded   gut-heavy

just imagining?

Pulvermühle
the German hamlet where I'm eight years old
and there's just two of us girls

      number 3 and number 4

and our mother is swelling against her wish
even we can tell

      but is this what is softening her?

dressing the two of us in dresses
mine a crisp cotton tartan red and pink and white
with a white scalloped collar

and we sit in a German field of daisies
making daisy chains and everything is soft and sweet

      and I feel like a real girl

then we're selling posies in the village market
and the peanut butter there is super-creamy-smooth
and what I don't yet know

      it will never taste the same again

you might say nothing much happened

there was no major incident

but how busy it was

all the nerve-sentries working overtime

attending to the possibilities

what if   what if   what if

if you said joy was elsewhere
I'd say go find it

but here
see what the camera snaffled
        who lies?

see the glossy colours the widening grins
pickled for keeps till paper rots

the rumpled pleats of memory
      which you want to iron out

smoothing out the press-lines
so that the skirt can fall simply
      gathered at the waist

the press-lines you want to iron out
smoothing the rumpled pleats of memory

so that the skirt gathered at the waist
      can fall simply

what authority does the once-child have
to speak from her adult mouth
like a hybrid bird of prey
preying on its own chick-self
cuckoo in the nest
cuckoo   cuckoo

      a gangly girl
      they call her *Goofy* because she trips
      and bumps things as she grows
      and she laughs with them laughing
      what else can she do

in the tiny brain how the fluids jostle

remembering, forgetting

tiny rivers
miniature brain-sized streams

remembering, forgetting

cloudy or clean swishing in the skull
sluicing the narrow rooms of the brain

remembering, forgetting

competing to save and banish

memory bubbles

                                    our father's special way with rooste
                                    crooning and cawing with them
                                    till they titter round his boots

            then the days there's the axe
            and the stained wood stump
            the chase the screech of rooster
            fresh blood on the wood
            that sweet-dank smell of wet feathers
            in the kitchen sink

                the satiny feel of my Communion dress

        the itch of nettles in the paddock
        but near the house a scent of roses
        and the climbing rose Peace pressing its face
        to the French window
        and when you stare into its petals
        the pink moves from pink to yellow to cream
                without a flicker

                                    an alpine meadow
                                    cowbells   gentians
                                    gentians blue as gentians
                                        gentians gentians
                                    the words ringing on my tongue
                                        like bells

and is it true?
can I see those little purple-black marbles
and taste their sweetness
and hear the urgent voices
        deadly nightshade deadly nightshade
and gag on the soapy swill
in my mouth
and hang on fast hang on fast to
those shiny berries
deep in my belly like treasure
        is it true? is it true?

the tock tock of the ping-pong ball on the ping-pong table and the talk that
bounces back and over the net with the white light ball that's like a tiny planet you
can blow around the sky and there's a laughing lightness to it all

                Point Leo my special birthday beach
                the one tree on the dune we claim our own
                the deep bright eye of the rock pool staring back
                and all its secrets in the depth of it
                anemone, crab, black spiky things, green lace
                and then the long long run along sand
                to the surf and all its dumping thrash and dive
                the rough scrape of sand on your belly
                at the end of a zooming ride

the landscape remarkably featureless
exaggerates us

the family exaggerated like an island
and like an island there's little sense
of joining any mainland

other humans and also animals are scattered
mostly out of sight

only some scraggy cats make it onto our island
never in the house and their kittens travel in sacks
again and again to the dam

and some spaniels wail in the distance

really the only marker is the sea's thin horizon line

so began my attraction to the minimal

memory
      like an echo
            you keep hearing
            keep
                  hearing

                  echo
                  echo

                        the sea's thin horizon line
                            horizon line

echo
      echo

under the bracken
                        bracken
                            acken

echo
      echo

                  zon line
                  line

                  under the bracken
                      bracken
                          acken

the great swill of stories you swim in
the countless hours and years recorded
contained in all the droplets

memory's vast weight of water behind you
pushing forwards
jump in   ride the current

       then the seductive voice of slower water
       there's too much   too muchness
       float here in my pool let the sediment settle

       the waters of Lethe beckoning
       the gentle sluice of forgetting
       purging the life lived
       readying it for the next

but not yet   not yet
memory the great river swirling on
insisting on its own trajectory
jump in   ride the current

brother, that weather round you four years old and banished to bed
so the two at the long table could shuffle their papers *thesis thesis*
a word they mutter and the pressure that even a child knows is an
interloping thing that pushes out all the other things and you refuse
to sleep and scream and scream and who is there perhaps two of
us sisters and he goes out and there's a booming fierce voice from
the side of the house near your window in the dark and a banging
on the glass and Agrippa announces himself out of the picture book
the whirr of his hair and his talons forever growing into the night
and your four year old bones no doubt shaking to a quaking stillness
the terror shutting your mouth silence silence and I know that a
wound is being bludgeoned into your veins and muscles and I feel
my innocence leaving this is what parents bequeath they who are
wise no longer and wrong it's all wrong and I who've been your
mother because others were not I'm now a girl growing towards
elsewhere but still I call myself guilty for not bashing down the door
or following Agrippa in the dark calling through the window *it's only
playing only pretending*

play play for the boy

he's much younger
keep playing every birthday

ring-a-ring o' roses

all of us pretending to be
children

a pocketful of

holding hands
jumping   falling

a tisshoo   a tisshoo
we all fall down

childhood such a small
discrete star
yet its rays searing

we all fall down

each of us piglets has to learn

where each of us runs out
where the others begin

don't touch   ouch

     and it's all frilly
     along the edge of a family's skirt

     you can fray there
     out of the toss and flick of it

     and learn to roll a cotton thread on
     your finger

on the fringe is the place for watching

can't you see, can't you see
I'm mouthing
can't you see, can't you see
I'm singing
can't you see, can't you see
I'm shouting

and what do I want them to see?

how his mood grows dark like sulky weather
how the house goes quiet and the air thickens

how his thunder rolls and cracks then the weather lightens
how we pretend nothing's happened

can't you see, can't you see
I'm screaming
turning the dial down to silent

can't you see
     there must be another way of being

but no one's hearing

don't stare too hard at anyone

don't look into their eyes
for more than a second

don't stand too close face to face
in case your eyes lock onto theirs

because

hypnosis is a sin
hypnosis is a sin

that's what the nuns are chanting

hypnosis is a sin

that's what the nuns are chanting

memory
>the great exaggerator

>plumped up
>bloated with fact and story

>booming out with its oracular voice
>*it was that   it was this*

>but agile too
>interjecting   interrupting

>flits   darts
>forgetting its weight

>slips into the queue
>insisting with a softer whine

>*it was this   I'm sure*

The house for all its walls is like a dream.
French windows have a way of streaming light,
how the brightness mostly makes our faces beam

but things aren't always what they seem.
Sure, I tend to dramatize our plight.
The house for all its walls is like a dream.

I face the wall that's red or black or cream.
Our dinner table places are set tight,
we all have fixed positions in the team.

Don't bother working up a head of steam
about the fact the distant sea is out of sight.
I have to trust the sun will make it seem

a swathe of blue, that special gleam.
Remember, how the sea looks is always right.
Meanwhile the walls no doubt have reams

of stories they could tell. Memory's like a stream
and other days it's like a tangled kite.
The house for all its walls is like a dream,
how the brightness mostly makes our faces beam.

just three of us
and a night storm no child
should have to conquer
the house about to capsize
from the battering of thunder
and my sisters wanting away
escape

so I give in to the march
the march through the dark
to a neighbour's patch
mad I think
to fling ourselves out
with the lightning bolts

but once in the dark
I smell the trees
they whisper *walk*
the gravel of the narrow road
pulls on my feet
this way   this way   walk

the surge of it
adventuring out in the blazing
flashlights of the sky
trudging the long mile past the gully
up the hill and down the hill
me the youngest leading
my heart thumping proudly
the night fierce and tender

how that nun keeps nagging

> *smile both sides of the mouth*
> *both sides now*

and suddenly there's Twitch

> *I'm Twitch*
> *flicking inside your cheek*
> *marking a sort of time a sort of beat*
> *ticking on the inside lip*
> > *twitch twitch*
> *gotta teach you life's not just smiley smiley*
> *not just a grinning game*
> *and till you learn*
> *I'll hide out in your cheek*
> *like a puckered stitch*
> *flick the switch*
> > *twitch twitch*
> *gotta be kind to be cruel*
> *or have I got it wrong*
> *whatever*
> > *twitch twitch*

> can anyone tell
> > can anyone see
> how Twitch is giving me hell

memory
        itself a sort of
        giddi
                ness
        as if there's
        a cliff
        one's been
        climbing
        and now
        looking back
        and down
        the vertig-
        inous dimension
        dizzy
                ing
        as if there's
        a cliff
        one's been
        climbing
        memory
        itself a sort of
        giddi
                ness
        and now
        looking back
        and
        down
        the cliff
        one's been
        climbing
        diz
                zy
                                ing

the German tea-set for visitors
white with blue flowers blue as gentians

the cups so wide and shallow
I need two hands to balance

please please don't fill my cup to brimming

the china so thin and light it's almost weightless
shows my shaking

please please don't fill my cup to brimming

the lip so fine my teeth might break it
the lip so fine my lips are slipping

please please don't fill my cup to brimming

       decades on with all the sorting and weighing
       of what matters and what doesn't

       please please don't fill my cup to brimming

       the tea-set's rushed into a carton
       and I stamp my foot like I'm seven

       hey let me tell my story
       how these cups scared me shitless
       how fragile how beautiful how wobbly

       please please don't fill my cup to brimming

all the unsung mothers

how I swallow my words
when I could be singing

her silky English Oil of Olay cheek
for instance

        and her patience
patience such a pale thing never noticed

and once when she wears
that gold and black glittering dress
with the swooping neckline
the satiny scent of it all

        she dazzles

and sure there are holes

which by their quality of absence
cannot be spoken of

until finally she says
I'm not good at feelings

and something fills

my birthday is hallowed
with a special glistening
as if carved from Christmas tinsel
(it comes just after)

out of the desert of the year
the birthday flowers
like a rare plant

the morning starts funnelled into the parental bedroom a sacrosanct
precinct and ever since that odd rubber thing was discovered in
your mother's bedside drawer there's a smell of rubber when
you enter and the sweet musty smell of talcum powder bodies
in pyjamas nightie don't look too closely lean over eyes shut for
birthday kisses sandpaper *happy happy* perch on the bedside like on
a cliff edge all the sisters watching and the pile of presents already
you're counting sizing up shapes and then in the glare of everyone
looking you play the charade of weighing guessing *it's a … no …
a …* laughs opening and oohing all the time thinking have you got
it right the exact amount of *thank you thank you* surprise delight
smile smile kiss kiss *thank you thank you* the jolly twitch playing up
happy happy and then released from the sanctum the thrill you admit
it seeing the half-garland of flowers round your breakfast plate
never forgotten always summer so there are roses daisies gorgeous
colours scents then you all jam in the car to the beach checking
measuring who might spoil the day being prickly bossy sulky but
once there the day opens out and the great generous belly of the day
holds everyone in the one container which is the sand rock pools
sky and surf at your own special beach Point Leo and everyone
heads off where they want and the sun's baking everything so the
day is unbreakable and you and all of them too until red and sandy
salty you narrow again into the car to the fish shop crayfish for
dinner special special and the long red flutes you suck the sweetest
flesh from and thankfully the day can glide tiredly to its end nothing
broken and thank heavens too late to play *ring-a-ring o' roses* thank
heavens sleep with the salt still coating next day you'll return to the
unnoticed *happy happy* the desert thank heavens you whisper except
for … except for Point Leo and crayfish …

the two hands of memory

   remembering, forgetting

attempting to gather, to gather
but the tiny drops refuse to cohere
and wilfully slip away

   slipping through the fingers

then magically back they come in the shape of sweat
the shape of sweat droplets on a horse's chest

   remember? remember?

and the beads of sea-spray on a wrist

   remember? remember?

and how the moon startled with its whiteness
flaring on the one hen
crossing the road at midnight

we are told to sit frozen
this is Bach this is Beethoven
wait wait

the wind-up gramophone in its magic chest
a wooden box high as my waist

the outstretched arm above the whirling shiny plate
our father's hand steering, lowering the poised
needle and then
                    it jitters
          takes off on its own travels, skids
squawks like a trapped bird

then again the waiting
this is Bach this is Beethoven
coming coming

the nervous needle settling back
on the black disc

and we still strapped to stillness in our seats
dare not shift a knee, a foot

wait wait

and suddenly from the needle's eye
the bird's let out of its bulky cage
unleashed and soaring now

and sings
sings so we can melt

and sometimes we are simply girls
sisters dressmaking round the ping-pong table

a scatter of patterns, *Simplicity, Vogue*
tiny-waisted models on the covers swirling skirts

our fingers whooshing the tissue paper maps
with their markings *pin here cut here*

folding, smoothing the fabric over the table
flowers, stripes, checks or a plain deep red

the square slim cake of marking chalk snug
in the fingers, pins in the mouth, mumbles,

the one in charge with her sure striding scissors
fantasy of scalloped neckline, flounces

all the cotton reels and their colours, bobbins
the word bobbin has us giggling

the cheery *clop clop* of the sewing machine
needle pricking into the poplin

then *try it on   try it on*
squirms and sniggers, frowns, adjustments

pins and patterns and puffed sleeves
fantasy of silk and lace, décolletage

simply girls

our house has a cool white weatherboard look
hugs the ground like a lizard
its stumpy feet in tread with the grass and the dirt
we never think of fire
        beyond the chimney

and the flames?
they come along the road another midnight
on the back of the man who's howling like a dog
        the flames climbing up his collar

and our father throws a blanket and rolls him
bounces him on the back seat to hospital
how his groans must have jerked out of his mouth
on the potholes
        our father a hero

and my sister swears she saw it all, hearing
his *Help Help* that old man from the sand-pit
where did he go after? the horse always spooked
by the black mangled tin of his one-time humpy
        what was his name?

on the sandy track
between two roads
there's firstly the flat
and the only possible hazard
a snake or rabbit darting out
so I'm gripping tight, gaining
speed to an almost gallop
shouting to the wind the
gutterals of a German ballad
Mein Vater, mein Vater,
und hörest du nicht?
then a twist in the track
a crest, then plunging
in a steep descent to
rough cracked ground
sometimes mud that
slows   me   down
the words long blown
a clatter of piglets at the pig-
farm, the pony skittish as
a foal and I pat and croon
coax her past

       later, later going back
       what a short straight
       what a gentle slope
       barely an undulation
       that sort of childhood
       fabrication
       how the mountain rose
       from nowhere

                                                the same place

how the snake   in exactly

            never reappears   67

            how

                the

                    snake

                        never

                        rea-

                            ppe-

                        ars

                        in

                    ex-

                    act-

                    ly

                        the

                            same

                                pl-

                                    ac-

                                        e

how

        the snake never

                        reappears   place

                            in exactly

                                the same

sorting family photos
I have to stare this necklace in the face
its dropped beads its frayed string

      this business of looking past the pictures
        how when they move to colour the gloss fades

she says sifting the pictures
that the process doesn't affect her one bit
and I wonder why she bothers to offer that unsolicited

      my childhood face is always smiling
        but of course you can't see the twitch

or how I stop singing in the car
when my father says how nice

how the cheery horizontal stripes of their uncomplicated shirts
flattened their chests which were bubbling with breasts each sister
in her own rhythm and hers the most timid being newest and the
stripes made all this a simple process flattening and in the photo
her eye and her grin are fixed on the dog the one that joined them
briefly you can see the fixity and how the dog rescues her and how
relieved she is at his flag-waving tail

it's all about measurement
a mysterious thing
how grateful you are
or not
how we're all measuring up

and the pencil marks on the door frame
measure our height
four girls growing
and at a certain point
I start hanging back from
the too-high mark

and going through the doorway
is a complicated thing
and I dash through
not looking at the pencil stripes

and when I can't escape the
measure-up, told to flatten
and stand tall against the wall
don't slouch don't cheat

red-faced in the flutter of
attention half-wanted
but not this
not this

I practise going tiny
on the inside
not leaving any mark

then there was the watching, whole
minutes of it, whole time,
enough to escort my childhood to
its window …
Beckian Fritz Goldberg

centre stage is taken
so hide in the wings to watch the action
the costumes have all been chosen
so there's no secret dressing
just watching

and on the train I leave my sisters
to their windows
and watch the backs of houses flitting by
all the backyards with their jumble of kennels
guineapig cages and hoists of white
and grey washing, blankets flapping

the innards of houses spilling out
how they all look the same
from the speed of a train

a sort of watching from the wings

she knows what a child knows
which seems enormous

how people dance together
a sort of dancing

how they ignore the colours of
their bruises when they knock
each other accidentally

how colour-blind they are
a puzzling thing

We don't want to let our childhood down
Tua Forsström

jump into memory's waters

stay there a while
    and feel the skin swell

stay there too long and the skin will
    crinkle like seersucker

stay there longer and the body will bloat
    a sort of pickling in the river

not enough

        not
        enough
        not
        not
        not
        not enough
        to go
        to
        go
        round

round   *round*   *round*

        not
        enough

to   *go*   *round*

when the nun bends down
in her half-moon bib
not one hair peeping
from that white band on her forehead

when she bends down and says it close
quietly like a threat
her eye glassy behind her glasses
a faint breath of cabbage

when she says it close
        if you doubt you are lost

something sings
        yippee, now I'm found

eleven years old *now I'm found*
let off that jangling chain, belief

chuck that little red book
that keeps hammering
with its nonsense
about sin and all its sizes

now I've arrived in doubt-dom

        welcome, this is home

Heart on the wall
they say it's love
see he's smiling

but no one can keep living or loving
with their heart burst open like that
that hole in their chest
and in the wrong spot too

    his Heart's on fire with love

rays of flame shooting out from the core
so everything is burning up
and that means wounds always wounds
and burns hurt the worst we know

    Sacred they call it

but his hair's way too long and curly
the heat of his Heart would singe it
frizzy at the edges but no sign of that

wounds, always wounds, grisly
like his ankles hands oozing blood on the Cross
and that means death
wounds and death, always death

    stop following me stop chasing me

those Heart's rays shooting off the wall
fiery arrows

    love they say

Sunday
the church all new and modern
so blame the light
its brash blonde sweep across the wide nave
how it bleaches all the faces
lights up the blotches and hollows
offers no hiding for us four girls kneeling
up front in the honeyed pew

     no honey here
     no sweetness
     no candle flicker
     in cathedral shadows

and how the light blares
on the priest's balding head
the weedy strands of his hair
lights up his whole shambling shape
the loose cheek-flaps,
the exaggerated lower hanging lip

you expect a bulldog's drool
but instead he stutters
all of him in slow motion to slow the stutter
its spattered spit
a guttural gurgly drone of a voice
sputtering threats from the pulpit
threats and the threat of boredom
the gut-twisting threat of a giggle
ssss…i…i…nnnnn…ing
hhhhheeaththe…e…nsss

look at the fishbowl there
the babies crying
in the crying room
escape there
escape to the crèche
where the Holy Family on the wall
smiles down on mothers fathers
babes on laps
happy happy holy families
smuggle the jelly snakes

one day in the fishbowl
there's a family there too dark
for the fishbowl light
the mother solemn the father thin
he watching her like she might break
words I don't know yet like *madness grief despair*
hover somewhere near
the brutal light blistering their shapes

our own mother not here
a hhhheeeaaaththe…thennn
how the hard wooden edge of the kneelers
cuts into my bony knees
leaves its white scar line
and the gravel of the priest's voice
lacerating
yyyyour mmmmmother's a a a hhhhheathththen

but now Communion time
and number 1 with her plaits swinging
bobs up from the front pew
and the three of us follow
me number 4 hitchhiking there in the Communion
queue behind the plaits
the strong straight ropes down my sister's back
pulling me *follow me follow me*

      caught in the light rabbit-like
      knees wobbling
      the long wait
      the terror when I'm frontline
      just me

the priest in slow motion bending over
his long knobbly fingers reaching into the gold chalice
to extricate the Host
the perilous slow descent of the wafer
his own mouth opening wider
his lower lip hanging way down on his neck

      child open up wide wide
      (silent … stutter-proof)

grip the shiny gold plate with frantic fingers
sweat   slippage   fingers taut
tongue shaking on its bed of teeth
the giant snowflake slowly descending

Jesus' body become snow?
from the red gashes on the crucifix
become snow?

but the snowflake's not melting on my tongue
it tastes like paper   a paper cut-out
so I'm tongue-shovelling it onto my gum
and it wedges there
glug   stuck

don't bite the Host
you'll splinter Christ

can I swallow it   swallow it whole?
in the panic slinking back to my kneeling post
working my mouth   swallow swallow

don't gag
don't gag on Christ

our father in the back pew huge-hunched
out of the main glare the gleaming
does he look up
see his four holy daughters
each in turn gobbling Christ

is it his ledger of sins weighing on his back
or the sacks of kittens he's drowned in the dam
the weight of them

that keeps him there in the back pew
and keeps him moody grey
on the car run home

until lunchtime finds his voice again
and he blasts the pious fumes away
like he's spewing what he's heard
all that indigestible holy business

the table silent   all of us silent
our heathen mother's face freshly painted
in heathen colours wearing a saintly grace
she waits out his noise   serves up the roast

me number 4 biting on my lunch   the solid meat
pushing the meaty question round my teeth

> *what is goodness?*
> *where does it hide in the priest's mouth?*
> *where here at the table?*

half-wanting to leap on my father's saddle
and gallop off
the stupid sermon   the threats   heathen
unkindness

> *what is goodness?*
> *where does it hide*
> *in the brash church light?*

You know now your own life doesn't belong to you
the way a child defects into his childhood
to discover it isn't his after all
                    Mary Ruefle

and sometimes the others tell your story
their version and you don't recognise yourself

and you never owned a dog not properly
so you can't let it take you home and say
            this is home and this is mine

and that's what it feels like
when they tell you about your life and yourself
what they remember as actually true

and what you don't of course
what you don't know a thing about

They are all our mothers,
those little appletrees
                Robert Minhinnick

a lullaby of apples, Granny Smith and
Gravenstein, Red Rome and Jonathon
and then the green cookers the nameless
worker drones of apples and it's them
I'm closest to in my bed on the farthest wall
of the house and there's the cherry plum
first its blossom then the little red baubles
of its plums pressing up against the glass
and I'm thrilled I don't share a wall
with our parents' room like my sister does
a foot's width between their three dreaming heads
but she's the one who calls out in the night
there's something under my bed sure there is
yeah sure, there's only the thump thump
of a roaming roo and then I hear a possum
bite an apple and hear his greedy rasping sigh
so I tell my sister she's mad and how I'm the one
closer to the creatures but there's solid glass
between me and the wild and hardly wild at that
just unmown grass and the surefooted-tangle
of apple trees so I go back to dreaming with those
green cooking apples unnoticed until my time for
ripening comes, mine and theirs

memory bubbles

> how the incinerator shoots out a spear of glass
> how it arrows straight for my heart
> how the Virgin medal pinned there
> makes it swerve ninety degrees
> how my soul is saved
> *miracle! miracle!*
> how to live a
> saved life

> wafts of
> chicken manure and lemon blossom
> from the two lemon trees

my father's huge legs
making an arch in the doorway
dash through   quickly quickly
they might snap shut
a leg might wheel around
and flick a kick
play on his terms
the rasp of his sandpaper chin
play on his terms

> the lilac time of year
> when the burst of purple
> against the white chimney
> that side of the house
> has me drinking deep
> from the heady purple sweetness

that time I fall off at a canter
where all the boronia's growing
the tiny brown flowers
packing a punch of scent
I fly off at a swerve
my neck's scratched
my father says *could have been your jugular*
what if   what if   what if

Scout wearing out the grass
racing door to door
past the lilac back again past the lilac back
nipping heels border collie style
sent away   a nuisance

a thousand chickens make a lot of stinking
mud
our mother's gumboots bogged
so she leaves them there
reads *The Egg and I*
laughs

there's a boy his hair in a tangle
running through the roadside scrub
his clothes a bit lopsided
he has a look of running from something
but also free
has a look of animal cunning
they say a boy from a boy's home is missing
I keep hoping he keeps running
with his animal cunning

I was as virgin of death as they come

       except when I hear
       the rooster's last scream

and when I see that sack
being carried to the dam

but what was that hanging in the air
when my father warned

       what if   what if

       what if   what if

what else could it be but
death?

for all his bluster
and the looming shape of him
his eyes are soft and
brown like a dog's
not really wanting to frighten

and sometimes I know this
sometimes I don't

there's a hierarchy of apples and ranked lowest the windfalls
nestling in the grass their red faces growing ghoulish and the bees
fizzing and feasting on their juices but even windfalls have a ranking
like the neighbours a safe distance away down the hill and up and
over there are goodies and baddies windfalls and neighbours and
the family of blonde boys with streaky pale skin wispy ragged hair
get the bruised and buggy apples the word jail is muttered comings
and goings often a boarded-up look to the house and a mangy dog
comes out snarling and the horse I'm on skitters past quickly and
there's a little blue house set back from the road with cheery dark-
haired Italians spilling out and they get the fresh-dropped bugless
windfalls and sometimes they're allowed into the orchard to pick
the fruit out of the grass as long as they don't touch the trees while
the blonde boys can scoop up their box of buggy apples from the
gate and if I'm out by the road in my tank-stand gym then I try to
hide but part of me wants to go out and grin at them to make up for
my mother's ranking them the lowest but I'm too scared they'll ask
me how high I can climb and then boast how monkey-game they are
and show me and put me to shame

Davey's Bay right side of the narrow path there are
high ti-tree fences and we can see the holiday
mansions through chinks and bends in the sticks
lawns with sprinklers whirling, white verandah posts
white tennis balls, people in white shorts and skirts
laughing on the grassy court, the scrubby cliff edge
on our left then the first blue of deep water
steep descent to the yolk-yellow sand and the boats pulled
up ready to race, their owners checking ropes
rich throaty voices everything looks and sounds rich and
we jam our rolled-up towels close to our chests to
hide the frayed bits check the tide, if it's out the jetty's
too high for a dive so climb down the broken steps
barnacles crusting underneath, quickly throw off the
shirt and towel so no one sees our bathers and leap
past the fishing lines and floating bowls of jellyfish
let the deep blue swallow us
                              bliss

memory
        with its brackish cul-de-sacs
        the side pools the shallows
        where the flow's got choked

talk of river
talk of the bounteous
great mother of stories, abundant water

        but talk also of drought
        the *same old same old story*
        of ground drying out

and a shrinking puddle
shouting threats

        you might as well forget
        you might as well forget

that's the voice of Lethe
the brackish cul-de-sac

but surely it's not such a sinister game

memory's not so plangent and pie-eyed
prognosticating out of its indelible
writing

remember the players
how they love tussling, wrestling

see what they're playing at

       it was red
       no yellow
       no green
              it was ochre with square panels
              that swarmed with antlers
              deer stalked there
      oh rubbish

at the séance of sisters
          what's pushing their fingers
this way and that on the table
obscuring the edges of this fact and that

and blowing a misty breath
so the room clouds with petals
          petals of the past

a misty breath blowing them
          away

in the distillery of forgetting
there's a silence

like the inscrutable surface of a lake at noon
a mirror that glares back at the midday sun
revealing nothing

how much is swallowed
and secreted
in the lower levels

but this is not lake country
not even a muddied creek

so let me go back to the bracken there
that hides the pond wedged in the gully

black puddle more like it
that boasts russet algae on its rim

and the bracken rusting over it
like a loyal friend

to reach the black gully pond
walk down the paddock into the bracken

down the sandy slope that ends in a gully
and in its narrow cleft there's an oval pond
with pitch-black water and a frill of rust around its rim

and the water of the shallows is also copper-coloured
before it deepens, blackens

and sometimes on the slope there's a snake's slither markings
and ants busying themselves in circles

and sometimes there's the blue flash-wing of a dragonfly
a flicker of sky on the pond's black mirror

someone torched
our old relics, the child-scribbles

the furry things we'd clutched
        torched but without any flame

the childhood debris chucked
in a rubbish tip no doubt

        no flame but still searing

and then remember Lethe?

erase this life before the next
was the instruction

Lethe who points to the future
by forgetting

wash clean wash clean

No, No, go not to Lethe …
John Keats

the river that encircles sleep
and someone whispering

slim pickings   your story
hogwash maybe

rub it out to a stain
a stain on the rock
where the water once gushed over

no   no

go not to Lethe

not yet

the family gathers after a long interval

three days of being and doing together
a confluence of rivers   each of us paddling

familiar echoes   piglet squeaks
can you hear them?

oh that's just the latest toddler squealing
relieved laughter   the future

perhaps I've got it all wrong   I'll be screamed down
not likely   each of us talking so quietly

the wine runs low   unthinkable
and you can hear the father

the patriarch shouting from his vantage point
underground   *u n f o r g i v a b l e*

at least *he's* still shouting

watching the white

                    ping-pong ball

pinging back

                    and forth

sisters musing

                    how we played the game

in childhood

                    who played most and least

the ball still pinging back

                    and forth

untarnished

                    nothing coagulating

on its pure light surface

                    its white mini-cosmos

just the breathless

                    ball

        scam-

                        per-

     ing

           free-

                          ly

number 4 won't play horses any more
and she'll rear if you try to saddle her
ride her bareback and she'll buck more

but today this midsummer's day
there's hardly a hiss from *that* past, way back

just this vast wide beach
in perfect summer bloom

and once again like innocents
we string out in a line watching the surf

my toes itching with that first ever *ouch* of hot sand
the giggly tickle of the wave's frill

Notes

Constituent / memories ... from 'Faithful and Virtuous Night', Louise Glück, *Faithful and Virtuous Night,* Farrar, Strauss and Giroux, 2014.

In Greek mythology *Menemosyne*, the personification of memory, was characterised as a river and also a goddess (mother of the nine Muses). *Lethe* was one of the five rivers of Hades and those who drank from it experienced complete forgetfulness. *Lethe* was also the name of the Greek spirit of forgetfulness and oblivion (from various sources).

Mein Vater, mein Vater ... from 'Erlkönig', Johann Wolfgang von Goethe, 1782. Translates as 'My father, my father / and don't you hear?'

the first house that burns ... from 'The First House is Burning', Beckian Fritz Goldberg, *Never Be The Horse,* The University of Akron Press, 1999.

then there was the watching ... from 'The Weight', Beckian Fitz Goldberg, *Never Be The Horse,* The University of Akron Press, 1999.

We don't want to ... Tua Forsström, *One Evening in October I Rowed out on a Lake,* translated by David McDuff, Bloodaxe Books Ltd, 2015, p.61.

You know now ... from 'Replica', Mary Ruefle, *Selected Poems,* Wave Books 2010.

They are all our mothers ... from 'The Fairground Scholar', Robert Minhinnick, *King Driftwood*, Carcanet, 2008.

No, No, go not to Lethe ... from 'Ode on Melancholy', John Keats.

*

My special thanks to Ralph Wessman at Walleah Press for his generosity of spirit. And to my partner Harry Laing for his huge support in 'living with the work' and his editing help.

www.ingramcontent.com/pod-product-compliance
Lightning Source LLC
Chambersburg PA
CBHW030352200726
48286CB00013B/1116